Book 1
Python Programming
Professional Made Easy

BY SAM KEY

&

Book 2

Rails Programming
Professional Made Easy

BY SAM KEY

Book 1
Python Programming
Professional Made Easy

By Sam Key

Expert Python Programming Language Success in a Day for Any Computer User!

Programming Box Set #53: Python Programming Professional Made Easy & Rails Programming Made Easy

Table Of Contents

Introduction

I want to thank you and congratulate you for purchasing the book, "Python Programming Professional Made Easy: Expert Python Programming Language Success in a Day for Any Computer User!"

This book contains proven steps and strategies on how to program Python in a few days. The lessons ingrained here will serve as an introduction to the Python language and programming to you. With the little things you will learn here, you will still be able to create big programs.

The book is also designed to prepare you for advanced Python lessons. Make sure that you take note of all the pointers included here since they will help you a lot in the future.

Thanks again for purchasing this book. I hope you enjoy it!

Chapter 1: Introduction to Programming Languages

This short section is dedicated to complete beginners in programming. Knowing all the things included in this chapter will lessen the confusion that you might encounter while learning Python or any programming language.

Computers do not know or cannot do anything by itself. They just appear smart because of the programs installed on them.

Computer, Binary, or Machine Language

You cannot just tell a computer to do something using human language since they can only understand computer language, which is also called machine or binary language. This language only consists of 0's and 1's.

On the other hand, you may not know how to speak or write computer language. Even if you do, it will take you hours before you can tell a computer to do one thing since just one command may consist of hundreds or thousands of 1's and 0's. If you translate one letter in the human alphabet to them, you will get two or three 1's or 0's in return. Just imagine how many 1's and 0's you will need to memorize if you translate a sentence to computer language.

Assembly or Low Level Programming Language

In order to overcome that language barrier, programmers have developed assemblers. Assemblers act as translators between a human and a computer.

However, assemblers cannot comprehend human language. They can only translate binary language to assembly language and vice versa. So, in order to make use of assemblers, programmers need to learn their language, which is also called a low level language.

Unfortunately, assembly language is difficult to learn and memorize. Assembly language consists of words made from mnemonics that only computer experts know. And for one to just make the computer display something to the screen, a programmer needs to type a lot of those words.

High Level Programming Language

Another solution was developed, and that was high level programming languages such as C++, Java, and Python. High level programming languages act as a translator for humans and assembly language or humans to computer language.

Unlike assembly language (or low level language), high level programming languages are easier to understand since they commonly use English words instead of mnemonics. With it, you can also write shorter lines of codes since they already provide commonly used functions that are shortened into one or two keywords.

If you take one command or method in Python and translate it to assembly language, you will have long lines of codes. If you translate it to computer language, you will have thousands of lines composed of 1's and 0's.

In a nutshell, high level programming languages like Python are just translators for humans and computers to understand each other. In order for computers to do something for humans, they need to talk or instruct them via programming languages.

Many high level languages are available today. Among the rest, Python is one of the easiest languages to learn. In the next chapter, you will learn how to speak and write with Python language for your computer to do your bidding.

Chapter 2: Getting Prepped Up

On the previous chapter, you have learned the purpose of programming languages. By choosing this book, you have already decided that Python is the language that you want to use to make your programs. In this chapter, your learning of speaking, writing, and using this language starts.

You, Python, and Your Computer

Before you start writing, take a moment to understand the relationship between you, the programming language, and the computer. Imagine that you are a restaurant manager, and you have hired two foreign guys to cook for the restaurant, which is the program you want to create. The diners in your restaurant are the users of your program.

The first guy is the chef who only knows one language that you do not know. He follows recipes to the letter, and he does not care if the recipe includes him jumping off the cliff. That guy is your computer.

The second guy is the chef's personal translator who will translate the language you speak or write, which is Python, to the language the chef knows. This translator is strict and does not tolerate typos in the recipes he translates. If he finds any mistake, he will tell it right to your face, walk away with the chef, and leave things undone.

He also does not care if the recipe tells the chef to run on circles until he dies. That is how they work. This guy is your programming language.

Since it is a hassle to tell them the recipe while they cook, you decided to write a recipe book instead. That will be your program's code that the translator will read to the chef.

Installing Python

You got two things to get to program in Python. First, get the latest release of Python. Go to this website: https://www.python.org/downloads/.

Download Python 3.4.2 or anything newer than that. Install it. Take note of the directory where you will install Python.

Once you are done with the installation, you must get a source code editor. It is recommended that you get Notepad++. If you already have a source code editor, no need to install Notepad++, too. To download Notepad++, go to: http://www.notepad-plus-plus.org/download/v6.6.9.html. Download and install it.

Version 2.x or 3.x

If you have already visited the Python website to download the program, you might have seen that there are two Python versions that you can download. As of this writing, the first version is Python 3.4.2 and the second version is Python 2.7.8.

About that, it is best that you get the latest version, which is version 3.4.2. The latest version or build will be the only one getting updates and fixes. The 2.7.8 was already declared as the final release for the 2.x build.

Beginners should not worry about it. It is recommended that new Python programmers start with 3.x or later before thinking about exploring the older versions of Python.

Programming and Interactive Mode

Python has two modes. The first one is Programming and the second one is Interactive. You will be using the Interactive mode for the first few chapters of this book. On the other hand, you will be using the Programming mode on the last few chapters.

In Interactive mode, you can play around with Python. You can enter lines of codes on it, and once you press enter, Python will immediately provide a feedback or execute the code you input. To access Python's interactive mode, go to the directory where you installed Python and open the Python application. If you are running on Windows, just open the Run prompt, enter python, and click OK.

In Programming mode, you can test blocks of code in one go. Use a source editor to write the program. Save it as a .py file, and run it as Python program. In Windows, .py files will be automatically associated with Python after you install Python. Due to that, you can just double click the file, and it will run.

Chapter 3: Statements

A program's code is like a recipe book. A book contains chapters, paragraphs, and sentences. On the other hand, a program's code contains modules, functions, and statements. Modules are like chapters that contain the recipes for a full course meal. Procedures or functions are like paragraphs or sections that contain recipes. Statements are like the sentences or steps in a recipe. To code a program with Python, you must learn how to write statements.

Statements

Statements are the building blocks of your program. Each statement in Python contains one instruction that your computer will follow. In comparison to a sentence, statements are like imperative sentences, which are sentences that are used to issue commands or requests. Unlike sentences, Python, or programming languages in general, has a different syntax or structure.

For example, type the statement below on the interpreter:

print("Test")

Press the enter key. The interpreter will move the cursor to the next line and print 'Test' without the single quotes. The command in the sample statement is print. The next part is the details about the command the computer must do. In the example, it is ("test"). If you convert that to English, it is like you are commanding the computer to print the word Test on the program.

Python has many commands and each of them has unique purpose, syntax, and forms. For example, type this and press enter:

1 + 1

Python will return an answer, which is 2. The command there is the operator plus sign. The interpreter understood that you wanted to add the two values and told the computer to send the result of the operation.

Variables

As with any recipe, ingredients should be always present. In programming, there will be times that you would want to save some data in case you want to use them later in your program. And there is when variables come in.

Variables are data containers. They are the containers for your ingredients. You can place almost any type of data on them like numbers or text. You can change the value contained by a variable anytime. And you can use them anytime as long as you need them.

To create one, all you need is to think of a name or identifier for the variable and assign or place a value to it. To create and assign a value to variables, follow the example below:

example1 = 10

On the left is the variable name. On the right is the value you want to assign to the variable. If you just want to create a variable, you can just assign 0 to the variable to act as a placeholder. In the middle is the assignment operator, which is the equal sign. That operator tells the interpreter that you want him to assign a value, which is on its right, to the name or object on the left.

To check if the variable example1 was created and it stored the value 10 in it, type the variable name on the interpreter and press enter. If you done it correctly, the interpreter will reply with the value of the variable. If not, it will reply with a NameError: name <variable_name> is not defined. It means that no variable with that name was created.

Take note, you cannot just create any name for a variable. You need to follow certain rules to avoid receiving syntax errors when creating them. And they are:

➢ Variable names should start with an underscore or a letter.
➢ Variable names must only contain letters, numbers, or underscores.
➢ Variable names can be one letter long or any length.
➢ Variable names must not be the same with any commands or reserved keywords in Python.
➢ Variable names are case sensitive. The variable named example1 is different from the variable named Example1.

As a tip, always use meaningful names for your variables. It will help you remember them easily when you are writing long lines of codes. Also, keep them short and use only one style of naming convention. For example, if you create a variable like thisIsAString make sure that you name your second variable like that too: thisIsTheSecondVariable not this_is_the_second_variable.

You can do a lot of things with variables. You can even assign expressions to them. By the way, expressions are combinations of numbers and/or variables together with operators that can be evaluated by the computer. For example:

Example1 = 10

Example2 = 5 + 19

Example3 = Example1 - Example2

If you check the value of those variables in the interpreter, you will get 10 for Example1, 24 for Example2, and -14 for Example3.

Chapter 4: Basic Operators – Part 1

As of this moment, you have already seen three operators: assignment (=), addition (+), and subtraction (-) operators. You can use operators to process and manipulate the data and variables you have – just like how chefs cut, dice, and mix their ingredients.

Types of Python Operators

Multiple types of operators exist in Python. They are:

> ➢ **Arithmetic**
> ➢ **Assignment**
> ➢ **Comparison**
> ➢ **Logical**
> ➢ **Membership**
> ➢ **Identity**
> ➢ **Bitwise**

Up to this point, you have witnessed how arithmetic and assignment operators work. During your first few weeks of programming in Python, you will be also using comparison and logical operators aside from arithmetic and assignment operators. You will mostly use membership, identity, and bitwise later when you already advanced your Python programming skills.

As a reference, below is a list of operators under arithmetic and assignment. In the next chapter, comparison and logical will be listed and discussed briefly in preparation for later lessons.

For the examples that the list will use, x will have a value of 13 and y will have a value of 7.

Arithmetic

Arithmetic operators perform mathematical operations on numbers and variables that have numbers stored on them.

> **+ : Addition. Adds the values besides the operator.**

> $z = 13 + 7$

> z's value is equal to 20.

> **- : Subtraction. Subtracts the values besides the operator.**

> $z = x - y$

> z's value is equal to 6.

* : Multiplication. Multiplies the values besides the operator.

z = x * y

z's value is equal to 91.

/ : Division. Divides the values besides the operator.

z = x / y

z's value is equal to 1.8571428571428572.

** : Exponent. Applies exponential power to the value to the left (base) with the value to the right (exponent).

z = x ** y

z's value is equal to 62748517.

// : Floor Division. Divides the values besides the operator and returns a quotient with removed digits after the decimal point.

z = x // y

z's value is equal to 1.

% : Modulus. Divides the values besides the operator and returns the remainder instead of the quotient.

z = x % y

z's value is equal to 6.

Assignment

Aside from the equal sign or simple assignment operator, other assignment operators exist. Mostly, they are combinations of arithmetic operators and the simple assignment operator.

They are used as shorthand methods when reassigning a value to a variable that is also included in the expression that will be assigned to it. Using them in your code simplifies and makes your statements clean.

= : Simple assignment operator. It assigns the value of the expression on its right hand side to the variable to its left hand side.

z = x + y * x − y % x

z's value is equal to 97.

The following assignment operators work like this: it applies the operation first on the value of the variable on its left and the result of the expression on its right. After that, it assigns the result of the operation to the variable on its left.

+= : Add and Assign

x += y

x's value is equal to 20. It is equivalent to x = x + y.

-= : Subtract and Assign

x −= y

x's value is equal to 6. It is equivalent to x = x − y.

*= : Multiply and assign

x *= y

x's value is equal to 91. It is equivalent to x = x * y.

/= : Divide and assign

x /= y

x's value is equal to 1.8571428571428572. It is equivalent to x = x / y.

**= : Exponent and Assign

x **= y

x's value is equal to 62748517. It is equivalent to x = x ** y.

//= : Floor Division and Assign

x //= y

x's value is equal to 1. It is equivalent to x = x // y.

%= : Modulus and Assign

x %= y

x's value is equal to 6. It is equivalent to x = x % y.

Multiple Usage of Some Operators

Also, some operators may behave differently depending on how you use them or what values you use together with them. For example:

z = "sample" + "statement"

As you can see, the statement tried to add two strings. In other programming languages, that kind of statement will return an error since their (+) operator is dedicated for addition of numbers only. In Python, it will perform string concatenation that will append the second string to the first. Hence, the value of variable z will become "samplestatement".

On the other hand, you can use the (-) subtraction operator as unary operators. To denote that a variable or number is negative, you can place the subtraction operator before it. For example:

z = 1 - -1

The result will be 2 since 1 minus negative 1 is 2.

The addition operator acts as a unary operator for other languages; however, it behaves differently in Python. In some language, an expression like this: +(-1), will be treated as positive 1. In Python, it will be treated as +1(-1), and if you evaluate that, you will still get negative 1.

To perform a unary positive, you can do this instead:

--1

In that example, Python will read it as $-(-1)$ or $-1 * -1$ and it will return a positive 1.

Chapter 5: Basic Operators – Part 2

Operators seem to be such a big topic, right? You will be working with them all the time when programming in Python. Once you master or just memorize them all, your overall programming skills will improve since most programming languages have operators that work just like the ones in Python.

And just like a restaurant manager, you would not want to let your chef serve food with only unprocessed ingredients all the time. Not everybody wants salads for their dinner.

Comparison

Aside from performing arithmetic operations and storing values to variables, Python can also allow you to let the computer compare expressions. For example, you can ask your computer if 10 is greater than 20. Since 10 is greater than 20, it will reply with True – meaning the statement you said was correct. If you have compared 20 is greater than 10 instead, it will return a reply that says False.

== : Is Equal

z = x == y

z's value is equal to FALSE.

!= : Is Not Equal

z = x != y

z's value is equal to True.

> : Is Greater Than

z = x > y

z's value is equal to True.

< : Is Less Than

z = x < y

z's value is equal to FALSE.

>= : Is Greater Than or Equal

z = x >= y

z's value is equal to True.

<= : Is Less Than or Equal

z = x <= y

z's value is equal to FALSE.

Note that the last two operators are unlike the combined arithmetic and simple assignment operator.

Logical

Aside from arithmetic and comparison operations, the computer is capable of logical operations, too. Even simple circuitry can do that, but that is another story to tell.

Anyway, do you remember your logic class where your professor talked about truth tables, premises, and propositions? Your computer can understand all of that. Below are the operators you can use to perform logic in Python. In the examples in the list, a is equal to True and b is equal to False.

and : Logical Conjunction AND. It will return only True both the propositions or variable besides it is True. It will return False if any or both the propositions are False.

w = a and a

x = a and b

y = b and a

z = b and b

w is equal to True, x is equal to False, y is equal to False, and z is   equal to False.

or : Logical Disjunction OR. It will return True if any or both of the proposition or variable beside it is True. It will return False if both the propositions are False.

w = a or a

x = a or b

y = b or a

z = b or b

w is equal to True, x is equal to True, y is equal to True, and z is   equal to False.

not : Logical Negation NOT. Any Truth value besides it will be negated. If True is negated, the computer will reply with a False. If False is negated, the computer will reply with a True.

w = not a

x = not b

w is equal to False and x is equal to True.

If you want to perform Logical NAND, you can use Logic Negation NOT and Logical Conjunction AND. For example:

w = not (a and a)

x = not (a and b)

y = not (b and a)

z = not (b and b)

w is equal to False, x is equal to True, y is equal to True, and z is   equal to True.

If you want to perform Logical NOR, you can use Logic Negation NOT and Logical Disjunction OR. For example:

w = not (a or a)

x = not (a or b)

y = not (b or a)

z = not (b or b)

w is equal to False, x is equal to False, y is equal to False, and z is   equal to True.

You can perform other logical operations that do not have Python operators by using conditional statements, which will be discussed later in this book.

Order of Precedence

In case that your statement contains multiple types or instances of operators, Python will evaluate it according to precedence of the operators, which is similar to the PEMDAS rule in Mathematics. It will evaluate the operators with the highest precedence to the lowest. For example:

z = 2 + 10 / 10

Instead of adding 2 and 10 first then dividing the sum by 10, Python will divide 10 by 10 first then add 2 to the quotient instead since division has a higher precedence than subtraction. So, instead of getting 1.2, you will get 3.0. In case that it confuses you, imagine that Python secretly adds parentheses to the expression. The sample above is the same as:

z = 2 + (10 / 10)

If two operators with the same level of precedence exist in one statement, Python will evaluate the first operator that appears from the left. For example:

z = 10 / 10 * 2

The value of variable z will be 2.

Take note that any expressions inside parentheses or nested deeper in parentheses will have higher precedence than those expressions outside the parentheses. For example:

z = 2 / ((1 + 1) * (2 − 4))

Even though the division operator came first and has higher precedence than addition and subtraction, Python evaluated the ones inside the parentheses first and evaluated the division operation last. So, it added 1 and 1, subtracted 4 from 2, multiplied the sum and difference of the two previous operations, and then divided the product from 2. The value of variable z became -0.5.

Below is a reference for the precedence of the operations. The list is sorted from operations with high precedence to operators with low precedence.

> ➢ **Exponents**
> ➢ **Unary**
> ➢ **Multiplication, Division, Modulo, and Floor Division**
> ➢ **Addition, and Subtraction**
> ➢ **Bitwise**
> ➢ **Comparison**
> ➢ **Assignment**
> ➢ **Identity**
> ➢ **Membership**
> ➢ **Logical**

Truth Values

The values True and False are called truth values – or sometimes called Boolean data values. The value True is equal to 1 and the value False is equal to 0. That means that you can treat or use 1 as the truth value True and 0 as the truth value False. Try comparing those two values in your interpreter. Code the following:

True == 1

False == 0

The interpreter will return a value of True – meaning, you can interchange them in case a situation arises. However, it is advisable that that you use them like that sparingly.

Another thing you should remember is that the value True and False are case sensitive. True != TRUE or False != false. Aside from that, True and False are Python keywords. You cannot create variables named after them.

You might be wondering about the use of truth values in programming. The answer is, you can use them to control your programs using conditional or flow control tools. With them, you can make your program execute statements when a certain condition arises. And that will be discussed on the next chapter.

Chapter 6: Functions, Flow Control, and User Input

With statements, you have learned to tell instructions to the computer using Pythons. As of now, all you know is how to assign variables and manipulate expressions. And the only command you know is print. Do you think you can make a decent program with those alone? Maybe, but you do not need to rack your brains thinking of one.

In this chapter, you will learn about functions and flow control. This time, you will need to leave the interpreter or Interactive mode. Open your source code editor since you will be programming blocks of codes during this section.

Functions

Statements are like sentences in a book or steps in a recipe. On the other hand, functions are like paragraphs or a recipe in a recipe book. Functions are blocks of code with multiple statements that will perform a specific goal or goals when executed. Below is an example:

def recipe1():

> **print("Fried Fish Recipe")**
>
> **print("Ingredients:")**
>
> **print("Fish")**
>
> **print("Salt")**
>
> **print("Steps:")**
>
> **print("1. Rub salt on fish.")**
>
> **print("2. Fry fish.")**
>
> **print("3. Serve.")**

The function's purpose is to print the recipe for Fried Fish. To create a function, you will need to type the keyword def (for define) then the name of the function. In the example, the name of the function is recipe1. The parentheses are important to be present there. It has its purpose, but for now, leave it alone.

After the parentheses, a colon was placed. The colon signifies that a code block will be under the function.

To include statements inside that code block, you must indent it. In the example, one indentation or tab was used. To prevent encountering errors, make sure that all the statements are aligned and have the same number of indentations.

To end the code block for the function, all you need is to type a statement that has the same indentation level of the function declaration.

By the way, all the statements inside a function code block will not be executed until the function is called or invoked. To invoke the function, all you need is to call it using its name. To invoke the function recipe1, type this:

recipe1()

And that is how simple functions work.

Flow Control

It is sad that only one recipe can be displayed by the sample function. It would be great if your program can display more recipes. And letting the user choose the recipe that they want to be displayed on the program would be cool. But how can you do that?

You can do that by using flow control tools in Python. With them, you can direct your program to do something if certain conditions are met. In the case of the recipe listing program, you can apply flow control and let them see the recipes by requesting it.

If Statement

The simplest control flow tool you can use for this type of project is the if statement. Have you been wondering about truth values? Now, you can use them with if statements.

An *if statement* is like a program roadblock. If the current condition of your program satisfies its requirements, then it will let it access the block of statements within it. It is like a function with no names, and instead of being invoked to work, it needs you to satisfy the conditions set to it. For example:

a = 2

if a == 2:

> **print("You satisfied the condition!")**

> **print("This is another statement that will be executed!")**

if a == (1 + 1):

> **print("You satisfied the condition again!")**

> **print("I will display the recipe for Fried Fish!")**

> **recipe1()**

If you will translate the first if statement in English, it will mean that: if variable a is equals to 2, then print the sentence inside the parentheses. Another way to translate it is: if the comparison between variable a and the number 2 returns True, then print the sentence inside the parentheses.

As you can see, the colon is there and the statements below the if statement are indented, too. It really is like a function.

User Input

You can now control the flow of your program and create functions. Now, about the recipe program, how can the user choose the recipe he wants to view? That can be done by using the input() command. You can use it like this:

a = input("Type your choice here and press enter: ")

Once Python executes that line, it will stop executing statements. And provide a prompt that says "Type your choice here: ". During that moment, the user will be given a chance to type something in the program. If the user press enter, Python will store and assign the characters the user typed on the program to variable a. Once that process is done, Python will resume executing the statements after the input statement.

In some cases, programmers use the input command to pause the program and wait for the user to press enter. You can do that by just placing input() on a line.

With that, you can make a program that can capture user input and can change its flow whenever it gets the right values from the user. You can create a recipe program that allows users to choose the recipe they want. Here is the code. Analyze it. And use the things you have learned to improve it. Good luck.

print("Enter the number of the recipe you want to read.")

print("1 - Fried Fish")

print("2 - Fried Egg")

print("Enter any character to Exit")

choice = input("Type a Number and Press Enter: ")

if choice == "1":

    print("Fried Fish Recipe")

    print("Ingredients:")

    print("Fish")

```
        print("Salt")

        print("Steps:")

        print("1. Rub salt on fish.")

        print("2. Fry fish.")

        print("3. Serve.")

        pause = input("Press enter when you are done reading.")


if choice == "2":

        print("Fried Egg Recipe")

        print("Ingredients:")

        print("Egg")

        print("Salt")

        print("Steps:")

        print("1. Fry egg.")

        print("2. Sprinkle Salt.")

        print("3. Serve.")

        pause = input("Press enter when you are done reading.")
```

Conclusion

Thank you again for purchasing this book!

I hope this book was able to help you to learn the basics of Python programming.

The next step is to learn more about Python! You should have expected that coming.

Kidding aside, with the current knowledge you have in Python programming, you can make any programs like that with ease. But of course, there are still lots of things you need to learn about the language such as loops, classes, and etcetera.

Finally, if you enjoyed this book, please take the time to share your thoughts and post a review on Amazon. We do our best to reach out to readers and provide the best value we can. Your positive review will help us achieve that. It'd be greatly appreciated!

Thank you and good luck!

Book 2

Rails Programming
Professional Made Easy

By Sam Key

*Expert Rails Programming Success
In A Day For Any Computer User!*

Programming Box Set #53: Python Programming Professional Made Easy & Rails Programming Made Easy

Table Of Contents

Introduction

I want to thank you and congratulate you for purchasing the book, "insert book title here Professional Rails Programming Made Easy: Expert Rails Programming Success In A Day For Any Computer User!"

This book contains proven steps and strategies on how to learn the program Ruby on Rails and immediately create an application by applying the rudiments of this platform.

Rails is one of the newest and most popular platforms. Thanks to the growth of Internet, this platform has been targeting audiences that are quite interested in creating stable web designs. If your work involves the Internet and you want to implement ideas that would help you launch projects online, you would definitely want to learn how to code using this program. Within this book are everything that you need to learn from installing the platform, getting the basics and making sure that you are ready to rock any programmer's boat.

Thanks again for purchasing this book. I hope you enjoy it!

Chapter 1 Why Rails Matters

If you are a computer programmer, the Ruby on Rails platform would probably the next program that you have to learn how to use. It is also worth looking into if your work is largely based on design, and you want to try something current to make websites easy to manipulate and beautiful. It could also be the platform that would launch your career or create leverage for yourself at the office. Yes, this platform could be your trump card to your next promotion, or that awesome site that you have in mind.

What Rails Can Do For You

If you are wondering what good this program can do for most computer users, then here are the awesome things that you can get out of the platform.

1. Get to Code

Coding is not rocket science, and if you are using Ruby, you probably would not even feel that you are using a programming language. You would want to learn to code to retain what you are going to experience with the platform, so take the time to study anyway.

If you are getting into Rails, you do not need to be a Computer Science major. If you are a businessman who has a great idea for a web app and you want to try coding it yourself, then this platform may be your best bet.

2. Get to Code Better

Sometimes it is not about arguing what is the best platform out there and get drunk arguing which is the best among Python, Java, PHP, or Ruby. If you already know other programming languages, you would need to still keep up with the times and learn some new tricks. Ruby on Rails provides that opportunity.

3. Get to Code Faster

RoR is a beautiful platform that allows you to write shorter codes, and it has a great set of features for exception handling which makes it really easy to spot and handle possible errors. You also would not need to still maintain the usual reference counts in your extension libraries. You also get awesome support using Ruby from C, which gives you better handle when you want to write C extensions.

RoR makes any programmer productive because it is opinionated and it gives guesses on how you can probably code something in the best way possible. The Don't Repeat Yourself (DRY) Principle of RoR also makes you skip the usual coding process of writing something again and again, which often makes the code long, complex, and difficult to debug. That means that at the end of the project, you get to look at your code and have a better grasp of what happened there.

4. Understand How Twitter Works

Yes, Twitter is created using RoR, and if you are an SEO specialist, a web designer, or simply a tech geek, knowing how this social media platform is done would definitely help you out. You would also discover that a lot of the hot new websites today are built on this platform.

5. Learn a Platform with a Great Community

RoR is relatively young compared to other programming languages, and for that reason, it has a very active and collaborative community. You definitely would get to hang out with several other developers and would probably build something together. Doing that is always good for your résumé.

6. It works with all operating systems and offers threading that is independent from the operating system. That means that is also very portable, and would even work on a computer that runs on Windows 95.

If these perks sound great, then it's time to get started with a Rails project!

Chapter 2 Getting Started

If you want to learn how to use Rails, then you would need to first have the following:

1. Ruby – choose the language version that is 1.9.3, or later. You can download it by visiting ruby-lang.org.

2. RubyGems packaging system – it is typically installed with Ruby that has versions 1.9 or newer.

3. Installed SQLite3 Database

Rails, as you probably figured out, is a framework dedicated to web application development written in the language of Ruby. That means that you would want to learn a little bit of Ruby coding in order to eliminate any difficulty in jumping into Rails. If you have a browser open, you can get great help in practicing Ruby codes by logging in to tryruby.org, which features a great interactive web tutorial. Try it out first to get the hang out of coding with Ruby.

If you do not have any working SQLite 3 yet, you can find it at sqlite.org. You can also get installation instructions there.

Installing Rails

1. Run the Rails installer (for Windows and Mac users) or the Tokaido (Mac OS X users)

2. Check out the version of the installed Ruby on your computer by running the Run command on Start menu and then typing cmd on the prompt (Windows). If you are running on Mac OS X, launch Terminal.app.

Key in "$ ruby –v" (no captions). After you hit Enter, you will see the Ruby version installed

3. Check out the version of SQLite3 installed by typing "$ sqlite3 –version".

4. After Rails installation, type in "$ rails –version" on Terminal.app or at the command prompt. If it says something similar to Rails 4.2.0, then you are good to go.

A Note on the $ sign

The $ sign would be used here in this book to look like the terminal prompt where you would type your code after. If you are using Windows for the Rails platform, you would see something like this: c:\source_code> .

Chapter 3 Create Your First Project

Here's something that most web developers are raving about Rails: it comes with generators, or scripts that are made to make development a lot easier by making all things that you need to get started on a particular project. Among these scripts is the new application generator, which gives you the foundation you need for a new Rails app so you do not have to write one yourself. Now that allows you to jump right into your code!

Since you are most likely to build a website or an API (application program interface), you would want to start coding a blog application. To start, launch a terminal and go to any directory where you can create files. On the prompt, type "$ rails new blog."

After you hit Enter, Rails will start making an application called Blog in the directory. It will also start making gem dependencies that you already have in your Gemfile bundle install.

Now, go to where your blog app is by typing in "$ cd blog".

What's in There?

Once you get into the directory, you will find a number of files that Rails have already installed by default. If you are not quite sure about what these files are for, here's a quick rundown of the file or folder functions:

1. app/ - this has the models, helpers, mailers, assets, and controllers for the app you just created. You'll be looking more at this folder later.

2. bin/ - this has the script that you will use to run the app. Also, this has other scripts that you will be using to deploy, setup, or run the application you are going to create.

3. config/ - this allows you to tweak the app's database, routes, etc.

4. config.ru – this is the configuration that will be used by Rack-based servers to run the app.

5. db/ - this would contain your database and database migrations

6. Gemfile, Gemfile.lock – these would allow you to tell the program what sort of gem dependencies you are going to need for the app you're building.

7. lib/ - contains the extended modules needed for the app

8. lib – contains the app's log files

9. public/ – this would be the sole folder that other people could see. It would be containing all your compiled assets and created static files.

10. Rakefile – this would be the one file that would locate and load tasks that can be set to run from the command line. You can add tasks that you would prefer to use later on by adding the files needed to the lib/tasks directory

11. README.rdoc – just like readme's function, this would be a brief document that would tell other people how your app works, how to set it up, etc.

12. test/ - these would contain all your unit tests and all the things that you are going to need for testing.

13. tmp/ - this would hold all temporary files

14. vendor/ - this would contain all your third-party codes and would also contain all vendored gems.

Now, if you are seeing all these in the app directory you just made, then you are ready to create little bits and pieces that you would be adding up later to make a real blog app!

Firing Up the Web Server

Since you already have the barebones of your blog application, you would want to set up how the app is going to be launched on the internet. To start a web server go to the directory where blog is located, and then type "$ bin/rails server".

Important note:

You would need to have a JavaScript runtime available in your computer if you want to use asset compression for JavaScript or if you want to compile a CoffeeScript. Otherwise, you would expect to see an execjs error when you attempt to compile these assets. If you want to look at all the supported runtimes, you can go to github.com/sstephenson/execjs#readme.

If you are successful, what you just did would launch WEBrick, which is the server that Ruby apps use by default. You can see what's happening so far in your app by firing up a web browser and typing http://localhost:3000. Now, since you have done nothing much, you would be seeing the Rails default page. It will tell you that you are currently in development mode. You also do not need to constantly require the server to look at the changes that you have made – any changes will be automatically picked up and seen. Also keep in mind that if you managed to see this "Welcome Aboard" thing, you are sure that you created an app that is configured correctly. If you want to find out the app's environment, click on "About your application's environment" link.

Got everything right so far? Let's move on to making something other people can read.

Chapter 4 Say "Hello There!"

If you want to make Rails learn how to say Hi to other people, you would need the following:

1. A controller

The purpose of a controller is to allow your program to receive any requests. When you route, you enable Rails to decide which of the controllers you set up will receive which types of requests. That may also mean that there would be different routes leading to the controller, which would be triggered by specific actions. An action is required in order to collect any information needed in order to send it to a view

2. A view

This thing's main purpose is to enable Rails to display the information made available to the action and display it in a format that other people can read. There are different view templates that are already available and coded using eRuby, which can be used in request cycles before it the information is sent to anyone who wants to look at this information.

Got it? Good. Now, to setup your welcome page, you need to generate a controller and then name it "welcome" using an action named "index". Your code will look like this:

$ bin/rails generate controller welcome index

Now, Rails will be creating a bunch of files plus a route for you to use. When Rails is done with that, you will see this:

```
create  app/controllers/welcome_controller.rb
 route  get 'welcome/index'
invoke  erb
create    app/views/welcome
create    app/views/welcome/index.html.erb
invoke  test_unit
create    test/controllers/welcome_controller_test.rb
invoke  helper
create    app/helpers/welcome_helper.rb
invoke  assets
invoke    coffee
create      app/assets/javascripts/welcome.js.coffee
invoke    scss
create      app/assets/stylesheets/welcome.css.scss
```

If you want to view where the course of your controller is, go to app/controllers/welcome_controller.rb. If you want to look at the view, you can find it at app/views/welcome/index.html.erb.

Here comes the fun part. Pull up a text editor and open app/views/welcome/index.html.erb there. Clear all the codes you see there, and replace it with this:

```
<h1>Hello Rails!</h1>
```

After doing so, you have successfully informed Rails that you want "Hello Rails!" to appear. That means that it is also the greeting that you want to see when you go to http://localhost:3000, which is still displaying "Welcome aboard".

Create the App's Home Page

The next thing that you need to do is to tell Rails where the home page is. To do that, pull up your text editor again and open config/routes.rb. You should see something like this:

```
Rails.application.routes.draw do
get 'welcome/index'

# The priority is based upon order of creation:
# first created -> highest priority.
#
# You can have the root of your site routed with "root"
# root 'welcome#index'
#
# ...
```

Those lines represent the routing file which tells Rails how to link requests to specific actions and controllers. Now, find the line "root 'welcome#index'" and uncomment it. When you get back to http://localhost:3000, you will see that it now displays Hello Rails!

Chapter 5 Let's Do Something More

Now that you have figured out how to make a controller, a view, and an action, it's time to create a new resource. A resource is something that groups together similar objects the same way you group people, plants, and animals. To make items for resources, you use the CRUD method (create, read, update, destroy).

Rails make it easy for you to build websites because it already comes with a method for resources that it can use for making a REST resource. REST, or Representational State Transfer is known as the web's architectural structure which is used to design all applications that use a network, and instead of using rather complex operations to link two machines, you can use HTTP to make machines communicate. That means that in a lot of ways, the Internet is based on a RESTful design.

Now, following the project you are creating, pull up config/routes.rb and make sure it's going to look like this:

```
Rails.application.routes.draw do

  resources :articles

  root 'welcome#index'
end
```

If you are going to look at the rake routes, you will notice that Rails has already made routes for all actions involving REST. It is going to look like this:

```
$ bin/rake routes
      Prefix Verb   URI Pattern              Controller#Action
    articles GET    /articles(.:format)          articles#index
             POST   /articles(.:format)          articles#create
 new_article GET    /articles/new(.:format)      articles#new
edit_article GET    /articles/:id/edit(.:format) articles#edit
     article GET    /articles/:id(.:format)      articles#show
             PATCH  /articles/:id(.:format)      articles#update
             PUT    /articles/:id(.:format)      articles#update
             DELETE /articles/:id(.:format)      articles#destroy
        root GET    /                            welcome#index
```

Chaper 6 Creating Article Title

This part would be the creating and reading part of CRUD, where you would put in a location where you would be placing articles for the blog you're building. In order to do so, you can create an ArticlesController by running this code:

$ bin/rails g controller articles

Now, you need to manually place an action inside the controller that you just created. Go to app/controllers/articles_controller.rb and pull up the class ArticlesController. Edit it to look like this:

class ArticlesController < ApplicationController

  def new

  end

end

You now have to create a template that Rails would be able to view. In order to create a title for the article that you want to display, pull up app/views/articles/new.html.erb and make a new file there. Type the following:

<h1>New Article</h1>

What did just happen? Check out http://localhost:3000/articles/new and you will see that the page now has a title! You will now want to create a template that will look like a form that you can fill up to write your articles in online.

Chapter 7 Creating the Form

Pull up app/views/articles/new.html.erb and then add this code:

```
        <%= form_for :article do |f| %>
  <p>
   <%= f.label :title %><br>
   <%= f.text_field :title %>
  </p>

  <p>
   <%= f.label :text %><br>
   <%= f.text_area :text %>
  </p>

  <p>
   <%= f.submit %>
  </p>
<% end %>
```

You will see that you have just created a form that has a space for the article title text, submit button, and it comes with boxes too! That is the function of the code form_for. You will realize that when you submit an article you are going to create, it needs to be done in another URL and then the entire text should then go somewhere else. Edit app/views/articles/new.html.erb by finding the form_for line and make it look like this:

```
<%= form_for :article, url: articles_path do |f| %>
```

In Rails, the action "create" does the job of making new forms for submissions, and therefore, your form should be working towards this action. You would notice that when you try to submit an article, you would see an error there. In order to make it work, you need to make a "create action" within the ArticlesController.

Create the Article

In order to get rid of this error, you need to edit the ArticlesController class found in app/controllers/articles_controller.rb. It should look like this:

```
class ArticlesController < ApplicationController
        def new
        end

        def create
        end
```

end

Once that is done, the controller should now be able to save the article to the database. Now, you would need to set the parameters of actions done by controllers. Now, make the ending of the above lines to look like this instead:

```
def create
  render plain: params[:article].inspect
end
```

Now that should make the error go away. Try refreshing the page to see what happened.

Make the Model

Rails already provide a generator that would be used by your project to launch a model. To order Rails to start generating one, run this on the terminal:

```
$ bin/rails generate model Article title:string text:text
```

What just happened is that you told Rails that you are requiring an Article model that has a title and a text that are attributed to separate strings. You would see that the platform made up a lot of files, but you would be most interested in db/migrate/20140120191729_create_articles.rb which contains your blog's database.

Now, you would want to run a migration, which you can do with a single line of code:

```
$ bin/rake db:migrate
```

What Rails would do is that it would be executing this command which means that it made the Articles Table:

```
==                          CreateArticles:          migrating
===================================================
-- create_table(:articles)
  -> 0.0019s
==          CreateArticles:    migrated    (0.0020s)
=====================================
```

Chapter 8 Save Your Data

Pull up app/controllers/articles_controller.rb and edit the "create" action into this:

```
def create
  @article = Article.new(params[:article])

  @article.save
  redirect_to @article
end
```

You're almost able to create an article! However, when you refresh the page, you would see a Forbidden Attributes Error, and would point you at the line @article – Article.new(params[:article]). The reason Rails is giving you a hard time is because it wants you to tell what parameters should be in your controller actions. That allows your program to be secure once you run it, and prevent it from assigning wrong controller parameters which can make your entire coded program crash.

To fix this, edit out the highlighted line in the error you just saw and change it into:

```
@article = Article.new(params.require(:article).permit(:title, :text))
```

Show Your Work

In order to make the page display your article, you can make use of the "show" action by adding it to app/controllers/articles_controller.rb. Add these following lines:

```
class ArticlesController < ApplicationController
  def show
    @article = Article.find(params[:id])
  end

  def new
  end
```

Now let's add some style. Create a new file named app/views/articles/show.html.erb and put in the following lines:

```
<p>
<strong>Title:</strong>
<%= @article.title %>
</p>

<p>
```

41

```
<strong>Text:</strong>
<%= @article.text %>
</p>
```

Refresh http://localhost:3000/articles/new and then you will see that you can create articles and display them!

Chapter 9 Make Your Articles Neat

Find a way to list all the articles that you are going to create in order to have an organized database. To do that, pull up app/controllers/articles_controller.rb and add the following lines to create a control.

```
class ArticlesController < ApplicationController
  def index
    @articles = Article.all
  end

  def show
    @article = Article.find(params[:id])
  end

  def new
  end
```

Now, to add a view, pull up app/views/articles/index.html.erb and then add the following lines:

```
<h1>Article List</h1>

<table>
  <tr>
    <th>Title</th>
    <th>Text</th>
  </tr>

  <% @articles.each do |article| %>
    <tr>
      <td><%= article.title %></td>
      <td><%= article.text %></td>
    </tr>
  <% end %>
</table>
```

Head over to http://localhost:3000/articles and you will see all the articles that you have made so far.

Tidy Up Some More with Links

You definitely need to create links for the articles that you have created so your readers can pull them up easily. To add links, open app/views/welcome/index.html.erb and then change it to look like this:

```
<h1>Hello, Rails!</h1>
<%= link_to 'My Blog', controller: 'articles' %>
```

Now, what if you want to add a link that would allow you to write a new article right away? All you need to do is to add the following lines to app/views/articles/index.html.erb to have a New Article link:

```
%= link_to 'New article', new_article_path %>
```

If you want to create a link to go back to where you were previously, add the following lines to the same file:

```
<%= form_for :article, url: articles_path do |f| %>
  ...
<% end %>

<%= link_to 'Back', articles_path %>
```

Chapter 10 Create Some Rules, Too

When you are creating a blog program, you do not want your users to accidentally submit a blank page, and then just land right back where they were without knowing what they did. Rails can help you make sure that doesn't happen by editing the app/models/article.rb file to look like this:

```
class Article < ActiveRecord::Base
  validates :title, presence: true,
            length: { minimum: 5 }
end
```

That means that the title should be at least 5 characters in order for the article to go through, otherwise it would not be saved. Now that this rule for your blog is in place, you need to show the blog user that something went wrong and that the form should be filled up properly. To do that, tweak the "create" and "new" actions in app/controllers/articles_controller.rb in order to look like this:

```
def new
  @article = Article.new
end

def create
  @article = Article.new(article_params)

  if @article.save
    redirect_to @article
  else
    render 'new'
  end
end

private
  def article_params
    params.require(:article).permit(:title, :text)
  end
```

What just happened is that you told Rails that if the user did not type in 5 characters in the Title field, it should show the blank form again to the user. That doesn't offer much help. In order to tell the user what went wrong, edit the app/controllers/articles_controller.rb file again and to cater the following changes:

```
def create
  @article = Article.new(article_params)

  if @article.save
    redirect_to @article
```

```
    else
      render 'new'
    end
  end

  def update
    @article = Article.find(params[:id])

    if @article.update(article_params)
      redirect_to @article
    else
      render 'edit'
    end
  end

  private
    def article_params
      params.require(:article).permit(:title, :text)
    end
```

Now, to show this to the user, tweak the app/views/articles/index.html.erb file and add the following lines:

```
<table>
  <tr>
    <th>Title</th>
    <th>Text</th>
    <th colspan="2"></th>
  </tr>

  <% @articles.each do |article| %>
    <tr>
      <td><%= article.title %></td>
      <td><%= article.text %></td>
      <td><%= link_to 'Show', article_path(article) %></td>
      <td><%= link_to 'Edit', edit_article_path(article) %></td>
    </tr>
  <% end %>
</table>
```

Chapter 11 Update Articles

You would expect your users to change their minds about the article that they just wrote and make some changes. This would involve the Update action in CRUD, which would prompt you to add an edit action in the ArticlesController and add this function between the "create" and "new" actions. It should look like this:

```
def new
  @article = Article.new
end

def edit
  @article = Article.find(params[:id])
end

def create
  @article = Article.new(article_params)

  if @article.save
    redirect_to @article
  else
    render 'new'
  end
end
```

To allow a view for this, create a file and name it app/views/articles/edit.html.erb and then put in the following lines:

```
<h1>Editing article</h1>

<%= form_for :article, url: article_path(@article), method: :patch do |f|
%>

  <% if @article.errors.any? %>
   <div id="error_explanation">
    <h2>
     <%= pluralize(@article.errors.count, "error") %> prohibited
     this article from being saved:
    </h2>
    <ul>
     <% @article.errors.full_messages.each do |msg| %>
      <li><%= msg %></li>
     <% end %>
    </ul>
   </div>
  <% end %>
```

```
<p>
 <%= f.label :title %><br>
 <%= f.text_field :title %>
</p>

<p>
 <%= f.label :text %><br>
 <%= f.text_area :text %>
</p>

<p>
 <%= f.submit %>
</p>

<% end %>

<%= link_to 'Back', articles_path %>
```

Now, you would need to create the "update" action in app/controllers/articles_controller.rb. Edit the file to look like this:

```
def create
 @article = Article.new(article_params)

 if @article.save
  redirect_to @article
 else
  render 'new'
 end
end

def update
 @article = Article.find(params[:id])

 if @article.update(article_params)
  redirect_to @article
 else
  render 'edit'
 end
end

private
 def article_params
  params.require(:article).permit(:title, :text)
 end
```

In order to show a link for Edit, you can edit app/views/articles/index.html.erb to make the link appear after the Show link.

```
<table>
 <tr>
  <th>Title</th>
  <th>Text</th>
  <th colspan="2"></th>
 </tr>

 <% @articles.each do |article| %>
  <tr>
   <td><%= article.title %></td>
   <td><%= article.text %></td>
   <td><%= link_to 'Show', article_path(article) %></td>
   <td><%= link_to 'Edit', edit_article_path(article) %></td>
  </tr>
 <% end %>
</table>
```

Now, to give chance for the user to Edit his work, add these lines to the template app/views/articles/show.html.erb:

```
...

<%= link_to 'Back', articles_path %> |
<%= link_to 'Edit', edit_article_path(@article) %>
```

Chapter 12 Destroy Some Data

No, it does not mean that you have to ruin the entire program you built. At this point, you would need to make provisions for the user to delete some of the articles that he wrote. Since you are creating a RESTful program, you would need to use the following route:

DELETE /articles/:id(.:format)   articles#destroy

This route makes it easy for Rails to destroy resources and you would need to make sure that it is placed before the protected or private methods. Let's add this action to the app/controllers/articles_controller.rb file:

```ruby
def destroy
  @article = Article.find(params[:id])
  @article.destroy

  redirect_to articles_path
end
```

After doing so, you would notice that the ArticlesController in app/controllers/articles_controller.rb will now appear this way:

```ruby
class ArticlesController < ApplicationController
  def index
    @articles = Article.all
  end

  def show
    @article = Article.find(params[:id])
  end

  def new
    @article = Article.new
  end

  def edit
    @article = Article.find(params[:id])
  end

  def create
    @article = Article.new(article_params)

    if @article.save
      redirect_to @article
    else
```

```
     render 'new'
    end
   end

   def update
    @article = Article.find(params[:id])

    if @article.update(article_params)
     redirect_to @article
    else
     render 'edit'
    end
   end

   def destroy
    @article = Article.find(params[:id])
    @article.destroy

    redirect_to articles_path
   end

   private
    def article_params
     params.require(:article).permit(:title, :text)
    end
  end
```

Now, it's time for you to let the user know that they have this option. Pull up the app/views/articles/index.html.erb file and add the following lines:

```erb
<h1>Listing Articles</h1>
<%= link_to 'New article', new_article_path %>
<table>
 <tr>
  <th>Title</th>
  <th>Text</th>
  <th colspan="3"></th>
 </tr>

 <% @articles.each do |article| %>
  <tr>
   <td><%= article.title %></td>
   <td><%= article.text %></td>
   <td><%= link_to 'Show', article_path(article) %></td>
   <td><%= link_to 'Edit', edit_article_path(article) %></td>
   <td><%= link_to 'Delete', article_path(article),
       method: :delete,
```

```
        data: { confirm: 'Are you sure?' } %></td>
    </tr>
    <% end %>
    </table>
```

You would notice that you also added up a feature to make the user confirm whether he really would want to delete the submitted article. Now, in order to make the confirmation box appear, you need to make sure that you have the file jquery_ujs in your machine.

Conclusion

Thank you again for purchasing this book!

I hope this book was able to help you to grasp the basics of Ruby on Rails and allow you to create a webpage based on the codes and processes discussed in this book.

The next step is to discover other applications of the platform and learn other Rails techniques that would improve your program design and integration.

Finally, if you enjoyed this book, please take the time to share your thoughts and post a review on Amazon. We do our best to reach out to readers and provide the best value we can. Your positive review will help us achieve that. It'd be greatly appreciated!

Thank you and good luck!

Check Out My Other Books

Below you'll find some of my other popular books that are popular on Amazon and Kindle as well. Simply click on the links below to check them out. Alternatively, you can visit my author page on Amazon to see other work done by me.

C Programming Success in a Day

Python Programming Success in a Day

PHP Programming Professional Made Easy

HTML Professional Programming Made Easy

CSS Programming Professional Made Easy

Windows 8 Tips for Beginners

C Programming Professional Made Easy

JavaScript Programming Made Easy

C ++ Programming Success in a Day

If the links do not work, for whatever reason, you can simply search for these titles on the Amazon website to find them.